GROSS JOKES

CANOPY BOOKS

All rights reserved. No part of this publication may be reproduced in whole or in part, or stored in a retrieval system, or transmitted in any form, or by any means, either electronic, photocopying, recording, or otherwise, without written permission of Canopy Books.

Designed by Deena Fleming

© 2020 by Canopy Books, LLC

13319 Poway Rd

Poway, CA

Made and Printed in USA

THE WORLD IS FILLED WITH ALL KINDS OF GROSS, GOOEY, ICKY, STICKY, AND NASTY STUFF. AND BOY, IS THAT STUFF FUNNY! THIS BOOK IS PACKED WITH GROSS PUNS, KNOCK-KNOCKS, AND ONE-LINERS, SO GET READY, BECAUSE THE GIGGLES ARE ABOUT TO START!

Gross, Creepy, and Crawly!

BUGS, SNAKES, SPIDERS, AND OTHER CREEPY-CRAWLY CRITTERS ARE ICKY, GROSS, SCARY...AND HILARIOUS! TURN YOUR SHIVERS INTO LAUGHS WITH THESE SILLY JOKES.

Q: Who always comes to a picnic but is never invited?

A: Ants!

Q: How many ants does it take to rent a house?
A: Ten ants!

Q: Why didn't the butterfly go to the dance?
A: Because it was a mothball!

Q: Why is a bee's hair always sticky?
A: Because it uses a honeycomb!

Q: Why did the bee get married?
A: Because he found his honey.

Q: What do you call bears without ears?
A: B's!

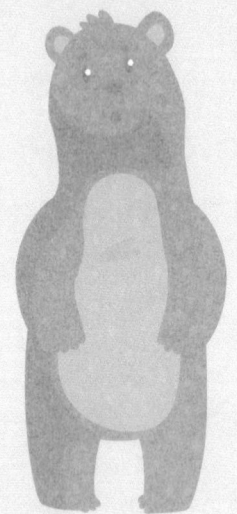

Q: What do you call a wasp?
A: A wanna-bee.

Q: Who is a bee's favorite singer?
A: Sting!

Q: What other singer is popular with bees?
A: Bee-yonce!

Q: Why did the bee go to the barbershop?
A: To get a buzz cut!

Q: What do you call a bee born in May?
A: A maybe!

Q: What kind of bee can't be understood?
A: A mumble bee!

Q: What do you get when you cross a race dog with a bumblebee?
A: A Greyhound buzz.

Q: What do you get if you cross a bee with a skunk?
A: An animal that stinks and stings!

Q: What does the bee Santa Claus say?
A: Ho hum hum!

Q: Why do bees hum?
A: Because they've forgotten the words!

Q: What kind of bee hums and drops things?
A: A fumble bee!

Q: What did the bee say to the flower?
A: Hello, honey!

Q: What did the confused bee say?
A: To bee or not to bee!

Q: What do you call a bee who is having a bad hair day?
A: A Frisbee.

Q: What do you call a bee explorer?
A: Christopher Colum-buzz.

Q: What is a baby bee?
A: A little humbug!

Q: What's more dangerous than being with a fool?
A: Fooling with a bee!

Q: Where do bees go on holiday?
A: Stingapore!

Q: What do you call bees buzzing in unison?
A: Stingalongs.

Q: What do you call a bee who's had a spell put on him?
A: He's bee-witched!

Q: Why do bees buzz?
A: Because they can't whistle!

Q: Can bees fly in the rain?
A: Not without their little yellow jackets!

Q: How do bees get to school?
A: On the school buzz!

Q: What's worse than finding a worm in your apple?
A: Finding half a worm!

Q: What do you call it when worms take over the world?
A: Global worming!

Q: What do you get if you cross a worm and an elephant?
A: Very big worm holes in your garden!

Q: How can you tell which end of a worm is which?
A: Tickle it in the middle and see which end laughs!

Q: What did the worm say to the other when he was late getting home?
A: Where in earth have you been?

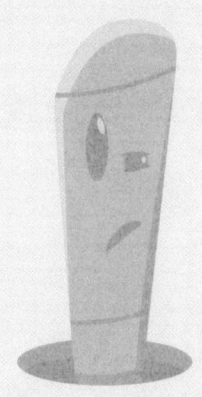

A man in a movie theater notices what looks like a worm sitting next to him.
"Are you a worm?" asks the man, surprised.
"Yes."
"What are you doing at the movies?"
The worm replies, "Well, I liked the book."

Q: Did you hear about the bedbugs who met in the mattress?
A: They got married in the spring!

Q: What is snake's favorite subject?
A: Hiss-tory!

Q: What snakes are good at doing math?
A: Adders!

Q: Why are snakes hard to fool?
A: You can't pull their leg!

Q: What snakes are found on cars?
A: Windshield vipers!

Q: What are a snake's favorite magic spells?
A: Abra-da-cobra and adder-ca-dabra!

Q: What's long, green, and goes "hith"?
A: A snake with a lisp!

Q: What is a snake's favorite dance?
A: The mamba!

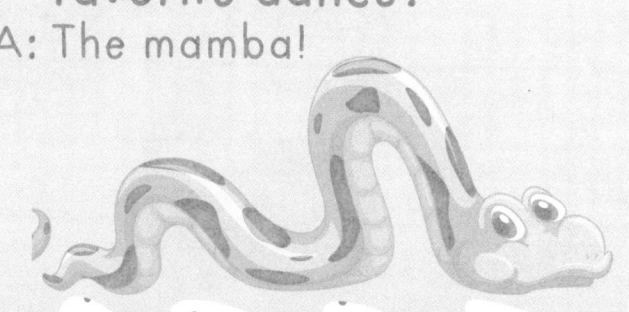

Q: Why couldn't the snake talk?
A: It had a frog in his throat!

Q: Why did St. Patrick drive all the snakes out of Ireland?
A: He couldn't afford the plane tickets!

Q: What do most people do when they see a python?
A: They re-coil!

Q: How do snakes put their babies to bed?
A: With a good-night hiss!

Q: What do you call a snake with a great personality?
A: A snake charmer!

Q: What do you get if you cross a serpent and a trumpet?
A: A snake in the brass!

Q: What do you give a sick snake?
A: Asp-irin!

Q: How do fleas travel?
A: They itch-hike!

Q: What do you call a snake who works for the government?
A: A civil serpent!

Q: What do you get when you cross a snake with dessert?
A: A pie-thon!

Q: What did the snake do when it got upset?
A: It threw a hissy fit!

Q: What do you do when two snails start a fight?
A: You just let them slug it out!

Q: What kind of slugs do you get when it rains?
A: Wet slugs.

Q: What has four wheels and flies?
A: A garbage truck!

Q: What do you get when you cross a slug with a rat?
A: The most disgusting creature you've ever seen.

Q: What do you call a dead fly?
A: A flew!

Q: Why did the fly fly?
A: Because the spider spied 'er!

Q: What do you call a fly without wings?
A: A walk!

Customer:
　Excuse me, there's a dead fly in my soup.
Waiter:
　I guess it couldn't swim.

Customer:
  Excuse me, there's a fly in my soup!
Waiter:
  Don't worry, he won't eat much.

Q: How do you make a glowworm happy?
A: Remove his tail—he'll be de-lighted!

Q: Why are spiders like tops?
A: They're always spinning!

Q: How do spiders communicate?
A: Through the World Wide Web!

Q: What's black, white, and red all over?
A: A tarantula with dandruff and acne.

Q: What do you get when you cross a huge hairy tarantula and a snake?
A: I don't know, but I'm getting nowhere near it!

Q: What do you call two spiders who just got married?
A: Newlywebs!

Q: What does a spider's bride wear?
A: A webbing dress.

Q: Why did the spider teen get in trouble with his mom?
A: He spent too much time on the web.

Q: What are spiderwebs good for?
A: Spiders.

Q: Who was the most famous baseball playing spider?
A: Ty Cobweb.

Q: Why did the witch's spider keep getting lost?
A: The leash was too loose.

Q: What's worse than a spider crawling into your mouth while you sleep?
A: Nothing!

Q: What happened when the man bit into a sandwich with a daddy long legs in it?
A: It became a daddy short legs.

Q: Why are spiders such good baseball players?
A: They know how to catch flies.

Q: What is a spider's favorite day?
A: Flyday.

Q: What do spiders order in Paris restaurants?
A: French flies.

Q: Why do spiders spin webs?
A: Because they can't crochet.

Q: What has 72 legs and catches flies?
A: A spider baseball team.

Strict Diet

A man feels itchy all over, so he goes to the hospital.

After examining him, the doctor gives him the bad news.

"You're completely infested. I've never seen anything like it. You have lice, ticks, fleas, and mites," he tells the patient.

"Oh my gosh!" the man replies. "What are you going to do?"

"Well, first, I'm putting you on a strict diet of pizza only," the doctor replies.

"How will that help?" the man asks.

"It won't...but it's the only food we can fit under the door!"

Snake Problems

An old snake goes to see his doctor.

"Doc, I need something for my eyes...can't see well these days."

The doc fixes him up with a pair of glasses and tells him to return in two weeks.

The snake comes back in two weeks and tells the doctor he's very depressed.

Doc says, "What's the problem...didn't the glasses help you?"

"The glasses are fine, Doc, I just discovered I've been living with a water hose for the past two years!"

Bathroom Jokes

IT'S A BOWL FULL OF LAUGHS IN THE FUNNIEST ROOM IN THE HOUSE!

Q: Why did the superhero flush the toilet?
A: Because it was his doody.

Q: What's brown and sounds like a bell?
A: Dung.

Q: If you're American in the living room, what are you in the bathroom?
A: Euro-peein'.

Q: What kind of soup do they serve in the bathroom?
A: Pee soup!

Q: What did one toilet say to the other?
A: You look a bit flushed.

Q: Why did the tomato blush?
A: Because he saw the salad dressing.

Q: What did one fly say to the other?
A: Is this stool taken?

Q: What do you call a magical poop?
A: Poodini.

Q: Have you seen that new movie *Constipated*?
A: It hasn't come out yet.

Q: How do you get the bathroom unlocked in a hurry?
A: With a doo-key.

Q: What would you find in Superman's bathroom?
A: The Superbowl.

I've always been told that life is like a roll of toilet paper. The closer you get to the end, the faster it seems to go.

Q: Why did the toilet paper roll down the hill?
A: To get to the bottom.

Boy:
  Can I go to the bathroom?
Teacher:
  Only if you can say the alphabet.
Boy:
  OK, abcdefghijklmnoqrstuvwxyz!
Teacher:
  Where's the p?
Boy:
  Halfway down my leg!

Q: Why can't you hear a psychiatrist using the bathroom?
A: Because the "p" is silent.

Q: What do you call a fairy using the bathroom?
A: Stinker bell!

Ewwwwww!

BOOGERS, BARF, AND TOE JAM MAKE THE GROSSEST JOKES!

Q: What's the difference between boogers and broccoli?
A: Little kids don't eat broccoli.

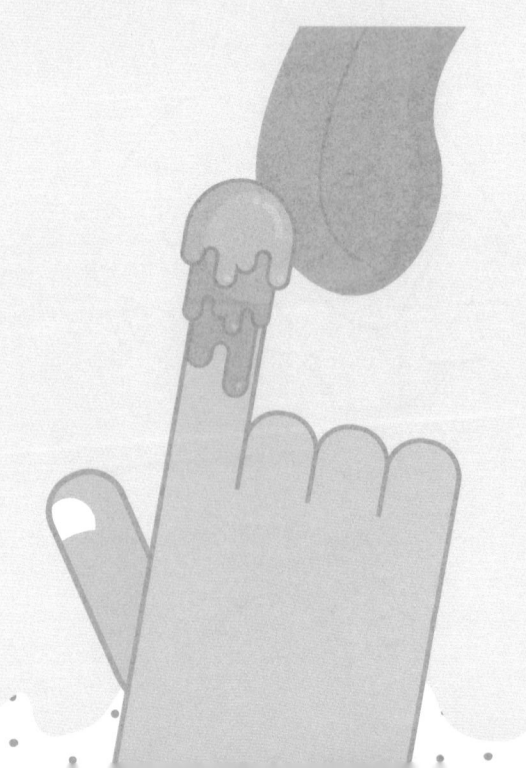

Q: Why did the booger cross the road?
A: So it wouldn't get picked on.

Q: How much does the average booger weigh?
A: Snot much.

A lot of people think boogers are funny
But they're snot.

Q: What do you do when your nose goes on strike?
A: Picket!

Q: Why did the man have to catch his nose?
A: Because it was running.

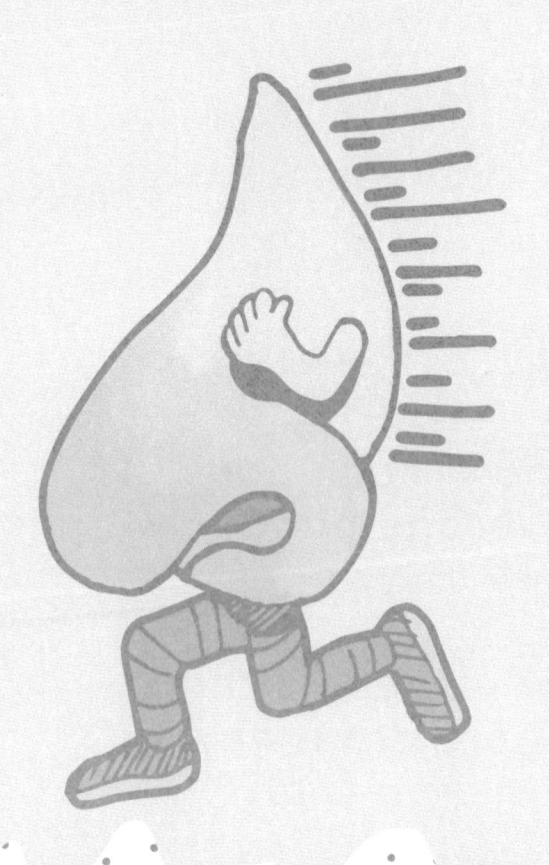

Q: What's another name for a snail?
A: A booger wearing a crash helmet.

Q: How do you make a tissue dance?
A: You put a little boogie in it.

Q: What does a booger in love tell his girlfriend?
A: I'm stuck on you.

Q: Where does your nose go when it gets hungry?
A: Booger King!

If you were a booger...
I'd pick you first.

Q: What do you call a skinny booger?
A: Slim pickin's.

Q: What do you call a sick reindeer?
A: Vomit comet!

Q: Why didn't the girl want to play basketball?
A: Because she didn't want to throw up!

Q: What do you call bread with your toe jam spread all over it?
A: Toest.

Q: What do you get when you cross a rock band with gross feet?
A: A toe jam!

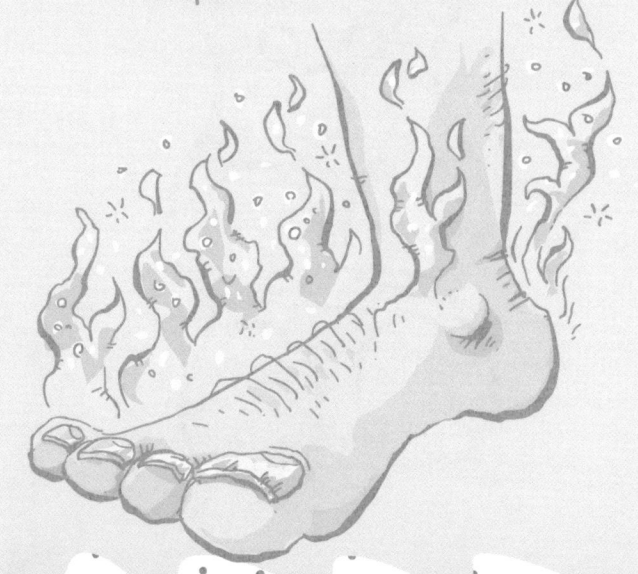

Sick Jokes

THEY SAY LAUGHTER IS THE BEST MEDICINE! SO TRY OUT THESE BODY PART AND DOCTOR JOKES IF YOU'RE FEELING GROSS!

Q: What do you call a bear with no teeth?
A: A gummy bear!

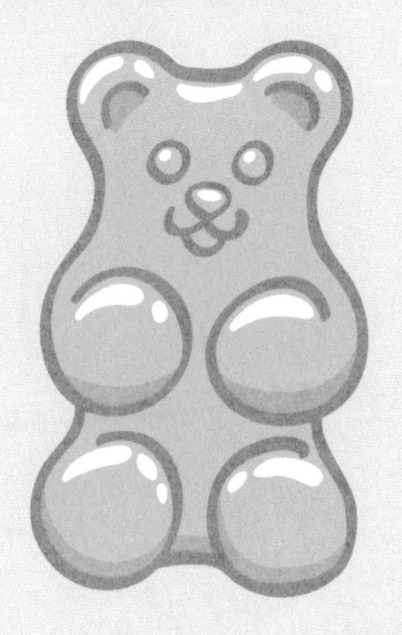

Q: How does a frog feel when he has a broken leg?
A: Unhoppy!

Q: What did one tonsil say to the other?
A: Better get dressed. The doc's taking us out tonight!

Q: What has a hundred heads and a hundred tails?
A: One hundred pennies!

I don't think I need a spine. It's holding me back!

Q. What do you give a sick bird?
A special tweetment.

Q: What kind of flower grows on your face?
A: Tulips!

Q. Why can't a person's nose be 12 inches long?
A: Because then it would be a foot!

Q: What has a bottom at the top?
A: Your legs!

Q: Why did the one-handed man cross the road?
A: To get to the second-hand shop!

Q: Why did the banana go to the doctor?
A: Because it was not peeling well.

Q: Why is your foot more special than your other body parts?
A: Because they have their own soul.

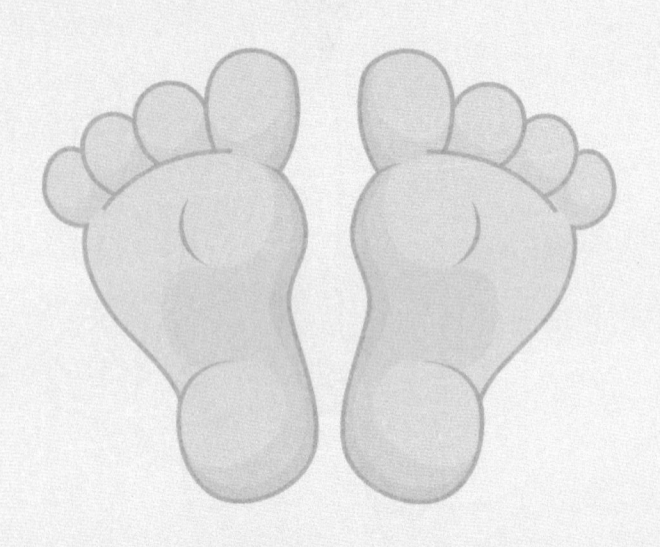

Q: Where does a boat go when it's sick?
A: To the dock!

Q: Why did the pillow go to the doctor?
A: He was feeling all stuffed up!

Q: Did you hear the one about the germ?
A: Never mind, I don't want to spread it around.

Q: Why did the cookie go to the hospital?
A: He was feeling really crumby!

Q: Why did the tree go to the dentist?
A: To get a root canal.

Q: What did one tooth say to the other tooth?
A: Thar's gold in them fills!

Q: Why did the king go to the dentist?
A: To get his teeth crowned!

Q: What did the judge say to the dentist?
A: Do you swear to pull the tooth, the whole tooth, and nothing but the tooth?

Q: What time should you go to the dentist?
A: Tooth hurty.

Q: What does a dentist do during an earthquake?
A: She braces herself!

Q: What did the tooth say to the dentist as she was leaving?
A: Fill me in when you get back.

Q: What is a dentist's favorite animal?
A: A molar bear!

Q: What kind of award did the dentist get?
A: A little plaque.

Q: Has your tooth stopped hurting yet?
A: I don't know, the dentist kept it.

Slime Time!

GOOEY, GOOPY GIGGLES ARE THE GREATEST!

Q: What did the baby slime say to its mommy?
A: Goo-goo!

Goo-goo!

Q: What did one slug say to the other slug who had hit him and run off?
A: I'll get you next slime!

Q: What did the slug say as he slipped down the wall?
A: How slime flies!

Q: What is tall, green, and has bolts in its neck?
A: Franken-Slime!

Q: What is slime's favorite game?
A: Slimon Says!

Q: What do you do with blue slime?
A: Try to cheer it up!

Q: What's the difference between a slime monster and a bucket of slime?
A: The bucket!

Q: Why was the monster so concerned when he found slime on his shoes?
A: He thought he was melting!

Q: What do you call two zombies up to their necks in slime?
A: Not enough slime!

Monstrously Gross!

THE MONSTER-RELATED JOKES IN THIS SECTION ARE SO FUNNY, IT'S SCARY! THEY'LL TICKLE YOUR FUNNY BONE FOR SURE.

Q: What do zombies call roadkill?
A: Snacks!

Q: What do you call a zombie's true love?
A: His ghoul-friend.

Q: How do zombies celebrate?
A: They paint the town dead!

Q: Where do zombies go to swim?
A: The Dead Sea!

Q: What does a monster call his parents?
A: Mummy and Deady!

Q: What's a zombie's favorite color?
A: Gangrene!

Q: What is a monster's favorite sweet treat?
A: Ghoul Scout cookies.

Q: Do monsters eat popcorn with their fingers?
A: No, they eat the fingers separately.

Q: What is the best way to speak to a monster?
A: From far away.

Q: What position do monsters play on soccer teams?
A: Ghoulie.

Q: Why did the slimy monster cross the road?
A: To get to the other slime.

Q: Why didn't the skeleton go to the dance?
A: He had no body to dance with.

A skeleton sits down in a restaurant.
The waiter says, "What'll you have?"
The skeleton says, "A soda and a mop."

Q: Why didn't the skeleton cross the road?
A: He didn't have the guts!

Q: How do vampires like their food served?
A: In bite-size pieces.

Q: Why did Dracula take cold medicine?
A: To keep from coffin.

Q: What did Dracula say about meeting his girlfriend?
A: It was love at first bite!

Q: What do you call someone that sucks the jelly out of donuts?
A: A Jampire.

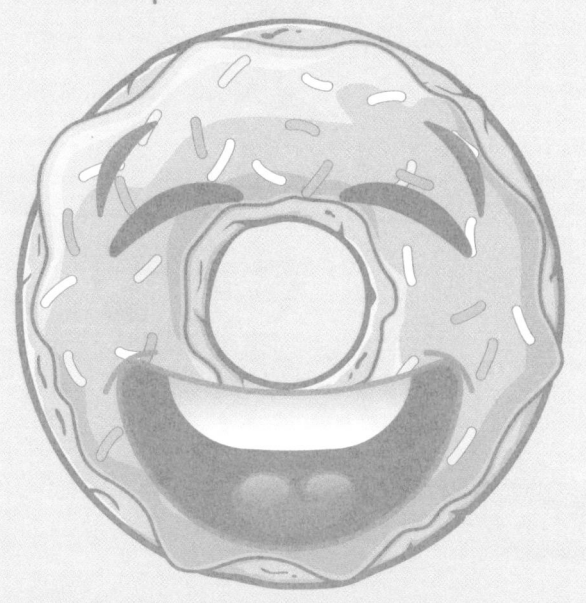

Q: Why did the vampire's head pop?
A: He bit someone with high blood pressure.

Q: Who does Dracula get most of his mail from?
A: His fang club.

Q: How did the witch say goodbye to the vampire?
A: So long, sucker!

Q: What is Dracula's favorite flavor of ice cream?
A: Vein-illa!

Q: Why did the vampire need mouthwash?
A: Because he had bat breath!

Q: Where do vampires keep their money?
A: The blood bank.

Q: What do you get when you cross a vampire with a teacher?
A: Lots of blood tests!

Q: Why are vampires tough to get along with?
A: Because they can be a pain in the neck!

Did you hear about the vampire who had an eye for the ladies? He used to keep it in his back pocket.

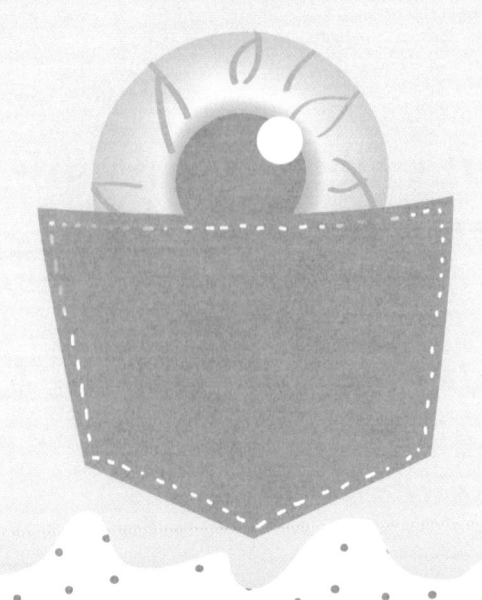

Q: Why are vampires easy to trick?
A: Because they were born suckers!

Q: Why was Dracula always willing to help young vampires?
A: Because he liked to see new blood in the business.

Q: What is a vampire's favorite sport?
A: Casketball.

Q: What did the polite vampire say after his meal?
A: Fang you for dinner!

Q: Which city do vampires in China live in?
A: Fanghai.

Q: What do you get if you cross Dracula with Al Capone?
A: A fangster.

Q: Why are vampire families so close?
A: Because blood is thicker than water.

Man:
Doctor, doctor, I think I've been bitten by a vampire!
Doctor:
Drink this glass of water.
Man:
Will it make me better?
Doctor:
No, but I'll be able to see if your neck leaks.

On the Menu

A monster walks into a restaurant.
"How much do you charge for dinner?" it asks the waiter.
"It's twenty dollars a head, sir," the waiter replies.
"And how much more if I wanted a few fingers and toes?"

Soup of the Day

A big hairy monster knocked on a witch's door and asked for something to eat. "You look familiar," said the witch. "Didn't I give you some bat's blood soup last week?"
"Yes," said the monster. "But I'm better now!"

Give Me Space!

ALIENS ARE JUST AS GROSS AS MONSTERS, SO TELL YOUR FRIENDS TO KEEP BACK WHEN YOU SHARE THESE JOKES!

Q: What do you call an alien who has six eyes?
A: An aliiiiiien.

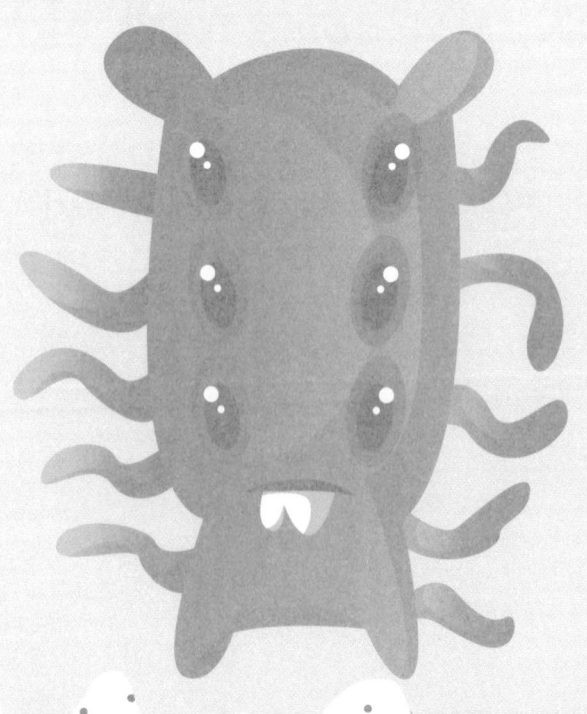

Q: What did the space alien say to the mama cat?
A: Take me to your litter.

Q. What do you give a slimy, gooey alien?
A. Lots of space!

Q: Why did the aliens need maids on their spaceships?
A: To clean up the cosmic dust.

Q: How do aliens keep their pants up?
A: With an asteroid belt.

Q: What do you call an insane space traveler?
A: An astro-NUT.

Q: What do aliens wear to formal events?
A: Space suits.

Q: Why did the alien go to the doctor?
A: He looked a little green.

Q. What do aliens use to build walls on the moon?
A. Moon beams.

Q. Why shouldn't you pick a green alien for your baseball team?
A. They're not ripe yet.

Q: How do aliens pay for coffee?
A: With starbucks!

Q: What was the space alien's favorite candy?
A: Mars bars.

Q: Why did it take so long for the alien throw a party?
A: It took a while to plan-et.

Q: What do you say to a 3-headed space creature?
A: Hello. Hello. Hello.

Q: What kind of crazy bugs live on the moon?
A: Luna-ticks!

Q: What do Martians serve their dinner on?
A: Flying saucers.

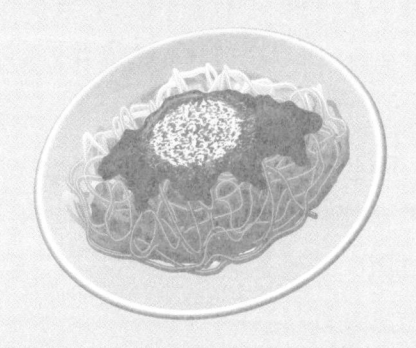

Q: Why did the aliens kidnap a wizard after they broke down?
A: They needed a flying sorcerer!

Q: What did the space alien like to read to her children?
A: Comet books!

Gross-Out Knock-Knocks!

YOUR FRIENDS PROBABLY DON'T WANT TO KNOW WHO'S THERE IN THESE ICKY KNOCK-KNOCK JOKES!

Knock, knock.
Who's there?
Seymour.
Seymour, who?
Seymour fleas in my hair?

Knock, knock.
Who's there?
Doug.
Doug, who?
Doug a hole for the latrine yet?

Knock, knock.
Who's there?
Sue.
Sue, who?
Sue me, I ate all the chocolate-covered ants!

Knock, knock.
Who's there?
Orange.
Orange, who?
Orange you glad you don't have worms?

Knock, knock.
Who's there?
Lettuce.
Lettuce, who?
Lettuce use the bathroom or there's going to be an accident!

Knock, knock.
Who's there?
Betty.
Betty, who?
Betty won't eat a slug!

Knock, knock.
Who's there?
Sara.
Sara, who?
Sara booger hanging out of my nose?

Knock, knock.
Who's there?
Tye.
Tye, who?
Tye a knot in that bag so the leeches don't crawl out.

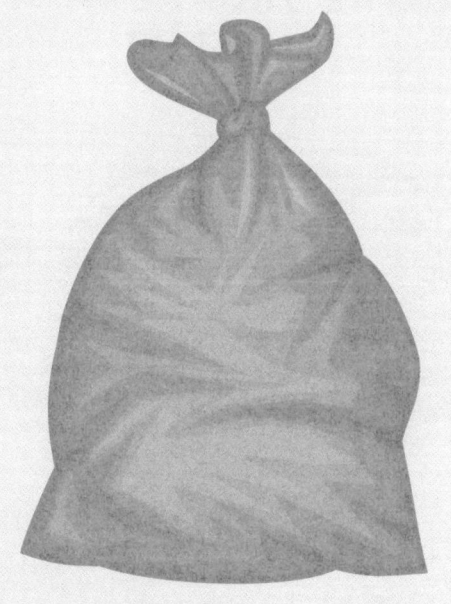

Knock, knock.
Who's there?
Canoe.
Canoe, who?
Canoe please stop picking at your zits?

Dirty Jokes!

THIS NEXT SECTION OF DIRTY, MUDDY, AND FILTHY JOKES WILL REALLY GET 'EM ROLLING ON THE GROUND WITH LAUGHTER!

Kid: I have a condition where I have to eat mud three times a day in order to survive...

Teacher: What??!!

Kid: I'm lucky my older brother told me about it, really.

Smart Potion

A kid is outside, selling drinks at a stand.

A man walks up to him and asks, "What are you selling?"

The kid says, "A smart potion. Would you like some?"

The man says, "Sure. I'll try some."

So the kid gives the man a bit of brown liquid in a cup.

When the man drinks it, he yells, "Blech! This is mud!"

The kid says, "See, you're getting smarter already!"

Eating Dirt

A vacuum salesman appeared at the door of an old lady's cottage and, without allowing the woman to speak, rushed into the living room and threw a large bag of dirt all over her clean carpet. He said, "If this new vacuum doesn't pick up every bit of dirt, then I'll eat all the dirt."

The woman, smirking, said, "Sir, if I had enough money to buy that thing, I would have paid my electricity bill before they cut it off. Now, what would you prefer, a spoon or a knife and fork?"

Man:
   "This coffee tastes like mud!"
Waiter:
   "Thank you sir, it's fresh ground!"

My son played soccer in the mud all day.
He was a little Messi.

City Slicker

A well-dressed man from the city breaks down on a country road. His cell phone is dead, but a kindly farmer tells him he can use the phone in his farmhouse, a few hundred yards from the road.

There is a very large puddle in the way, and the man looks at the farmer.

"Go ahead," calls the farmer, "it ain't deep!"

The man steps forward, and realizes, too late,

he's stepped into a very deep pond! He rises to the surface, spluttering, and hauls himself out of the water. He is now covered in mud and has slimy weeds wrapped around him. He's a complete mess.

He stands up and glares at the farmer. "Hey, farmer," he says, "I thought you said that puddle wasn't deep!"

The farmer raises his hand to mark a line across his chest and says, "Well, it only came up to here on the ducks!"

Q: Why does my son Richard like playing in the mud?
A: Because he then becomes filthy Rich.

I met a nun recently, she told me she always starts her day by rolling around in mud. I told her that's a dirty habit.

Q: Why did the chicken cross the road, roll in the mud, and cross the road again?
A: Because he was a dirty double-crosser.

Sick Pig

So there's this pig that's feeling under the weather. He goes to the doctor and says, "Doc, I've been sick all week, you gotta help me." The doctor pauses for a moment, considering options, and finally says, "Okay, this is an age-old remedy. Here's what I need you to do. Before you go in your mud pile, I want you to fill it with salt and sugar. Then, lay in there like you usually would. Call me in a week and let me know how you feel."

So a week goes by and the pig calls the doctor. "Oh, so how are you feeling," asks the doctor, "Better?"

"Better?" exclaims the pig. "I'm cured!"

Stinky Jokes

WHAT BETTER WAY TO END THIS BOOK THAN ON A REALLY FOUL AND SMELLY NOTE?

Q: Why does the giraffe have a long neck?
A: Because it has smelly feet.

Q: What do you call a stinky lawyer?
A: Law and Odor.

Q: What do you call an ant that doesn't smell bad?
A: Deodorant.

Man:
My dog doesn't have a nose!
Boy:
How does he smell?
Man:
Stinky!

Q: What did the judge say when the skunk walked in?
A: Odor in the court!

Q: What do you get if you cross an owl with a skunk?
A: A bird that smells but doesn't give a hoot!

Q: What do you call a flying skunk?
A: A smelly-copter.

Q: Why do skunks celebrate Valentine's day?
A: Because they are very scentimental.

Q: Did you hear about the skunk that went to church?
A: He sat in his own p-ew.

Q: What did one eye say to the other?
A: Between you and me, something smells!

Q: What do you call a cat that likes to eat beans?
A: Puss 'n' Toots!

Q: Why did dinosaurs take baths?
A: To become ex-stinked!

Q: What smells the best at dinner?
A: Your nose!

Q: Why is your nose in the middle of your face?
A: Because it is the scenter!

Q: Have you heard the joke about the skunk?
A: Never mind, it stinks!

A Tale of Two Skunks

Once upon a time there were two little skunks named "In" and "Out."

They lived in a hollow tree with their mother.

Sometimes In and Out played outside, but other times they played inside.

One day In was out and Out was in.

The mother skunk asked Out to go out and bring In in.

So Out went out, and in a few minutes, he came in with In. "My my, Out," she said, "how did you find In so quickly?"

Out just smiled and said, "In stinks!"

Paying the Bills Stinks!

A duck, a skunk, and a deer went out for lunch at a restaurant one afternoon When it came time to pay, the skunk didn't have a scent, the deer didn't have a buck, so they put the meal on the duck's bill!